AI Sales Accelerator

Convert Leads, Automate Outreach & Close Deals Faster

By Joe Correa

Published by Live Stronger Faster

This book is for educational and informational purposes only. The author and publisher are not engaged in rendering legal, financial, or other professional advice. Readers should consult a qualified professional before making any financial decisions.

First Edition

Table of Contents

Introduction

Artificial Intelligence is transforming the world of sales faster than any innovation in the past fifty years. In a business landscape where speed, personalization, and timing define success, AI is the new competitive edge. Gone are the days when salespeople relied purely on instinct, cold calls, and manual follow-ups. Today, the most successful businesses—large and small—use AI to predict buyer behavior, automate conversations, and close deals while they sleep. This book, *AI Sales Accelerator*, is your roadmap to mastering that transformation. Whether you're an entrepreneur, a sales professional, or a team leader, this guide will show you exactly how to combine the timeless art of selling with the cutting-edge science of artificial intelligence.

For decades, sales success depended on volume—more calls, more emails, more meetings. But in the AI-driven economy, success depends on intelligence. AI tools now allow businesses to identify ideal prospects with precision, qualify leads automatically, and create personalized pitches in seconds. Platforms powered by AI can scan your entire CRM, segment leads by intent and readiness, and even predict which clients are most likely to convert this week. Instead of wasting time chasing unqualified leads, AI gives you actionable insights that let you focus your energy where it matters most—on conversations that convert. Imagine having a virtual sales assistant that never sleeps, analyzes every customer interaction, and crafts perfectly timed messages to move deals forward. That's not a future vision—it's today's reality.

The beauty of AI in sales isn't just automation—it's amplification. When used correctly, AI doesn't replace human connection; it enhances it. It helps you understand your customers on a deeper level by analyzing their emotions, preferences, and decision-making patterns. It learns what type of content resonates most, what tone creates trust, and what moment is best for follow-up. For example, AI-driven CRMs like HubSpot, Salesforce Einstein, and Pipedrive's Smart Data feature can track micro-signals that humans overlook—such as response time, message sentiment, or browsing patterns—and turn them into sales intelligence. These insights allow you to build authentic, value-driven conversations rather than generic sales pitches.

In this book, you'll learn how to apply AI throughout every stage of the sales funnel. From lead generation to nurturing, from proposal creation to closing the deal, AI can cut your workload in half and double your performance. We'll explore how to use AI-powered prospecting tools to discover hidden opportunities in your market, how to automate outreach sequences that feel human, and how to integrate chatbots that book appointments, answer objections, and hand off warm leads to your team. You'll see how natural language models like ChatGPT can draft compelling follow-up messages, personalized offers, and sales scripts tailored to each prospect's personality type. You'll also discover how AI analytics can forecast your revenue, detect pipeline risks, and recommend the next best action for every deal—before your competitors even notice the opportunity.

But AI in sales isn't just about software; it's about strategy. Many businesses invest in the right tools but fail to align them with the right process. That's why this book combines technology with psychology. You'll learn how to use AI to enhance core sales principles—trust, empathy, and timing. For example, AI sentiment analysis can alert you when a prospect's tone changes, helping you reframe your response instantly. AI scheduling tools can find the perfect moment to reconnect based on behavioral data, increasing open rates and conversions. And AI-driven proposal systems can automatically generate dynamic offers that adapt to a client's budget and preferences. When these tools are combined with your personal selling style, they create a multiplier effect that turns effort into effortless success.

Over the next chapters, we'll break down each layer of AI-driven selling—from automation to optimization to prediction. You'll learn about chatbots that qualify leads 24/7, email writers that boost your response rate, voice assistants that take meeting notes, and predictive CRMs that act like your personal sales coach. You'll discover real-world examples of companies that used AI to 5x their closing rate and individuals who went from struggling with outreach to building entire sales pipelines on autopilot. The tools are available to everyone; the difference lies in how you use them. By the end of this book, you'll know exactly how to integrate AI into your workflow—no coding, no complex systems, just practical steps that any business owner or salesperson can implement immediately.

Most importantly, this book will show you how to keep the "human" in "high-tech selling." Sales has always been about trust, and while AI can help you communicate smarter, you'll learn how to ensure it never replaces authenticity. The key is using AI not to *speak for you* but to *amplify your best qualities*. You'll learn how to maintain personal connection while scaling your communication to hundreds or thousands of prospects. You'll see how to craft messages that feel handwritten, even when they're generated in seconds, and how to use AI analytics not to manipulate customers but to serve them better. The goal is not to turn you into a robot—it's to make your human skills more powerful, more precise, and more profitable.

The sales revolution has already begun. Businesses that adopt AI are closing more deals, reducing acquisition costs, and building stronger customer relationships than ever before. Those that ignore it risk becoming invisible in an economy that rewards speed and precision. The good news is that mastering AI in sales doesn't require a tech degree or massive investment. All you need is curiosity, the right framework, and the willingness to experiment. *AI Sales Accelerator* will give you all three.

By the end of this book, you'll know how to:

- Automate lead generation using AI tools and CRMs
- Personalize every message and follow-up at scale
- Predict customer behavior using data analytics
- Create chatbots and virtual assistants that handle sales tasks
- Build an AI-powered sales funnel from outreach to close
- Save hours daily while increasing conversions and commissions

This is more than just a book—it's a playbook for the new era of sales. It's your invitation to step into a future where every lead is warm, every pitch is personalized, and every deal is accelerated by intelligent automation. The question isn't whether AI will change sales—it already has. The question is: will you use it to change yours?

Chapter 1: The New Rules of Selling in the AI Era

The sales profession has always evolved with technology—from door-to-door pitches to telephone calls, from fax proposals to email follow-ups. But artificial intelligence has brought the most profound change yet. It's not just a new tool in the salesperson's toolbox—it's a complete reinvention of how selling works. The era of cold calls and generic emails is over. The modern buyer expects personalization, speed, and insight. AI gives you the power to deliver all three, simultaneously and at scale. The rules of sales have changed, and those who learn to leverage data, automation, and predictive intelligence will dominate this new landscape.

At the heart of AI-driven selling lies one principle: **knowledge replaces guesswork**. Every successful sale begins with understanding—knowing who your customers are, what they need, when they need it, and how they prefer to communicate. In the past, you relied on intuition and experience for this. Today, AI tools like HubSpot's predictive scoring, Apollo.io's lead insights, and ChatGPT's natural language processing can analyze thousands of data points in seconds to tell you exactly who is ready to buy and why. Instead of guessing which prospects to call first, AI identifies patterns invisible to the human eye—helping you focus your attention on the right opportunities at the right moment.

This shift also means the **old idea of "sales volume equals success" no longer applies**. The future belongs to precision. Instead of blasting hundreds of generic messages daily, AI allows you to send fewer but perfectly targeted communications. With the help of AI copy generators, you can craft personalized outreach that reflects a lead's exact pain points, tone, and interests. For instance, an AI system can review a prospect's LinkedIn activity, recent company news, and past email interactions to suggest a message that feels tailor-made—because, in many ways, it is. The recipient feels seen, understood, and valued, which is the essence of effective selling.

But AI's true power goes beyond writing or researching—it lies in its **ability to learn and adapt continuously**. Traditional sales training teaches scripts and closing techniques. AI teaches optimization. Every interaction becomes a data point that the system studies to improve future performance. Tools like Gong and Lavender, for example, analyze your calls, emails, and tone of voice to identify patterns that lead to conversions. They reveal which phrases generate positive responses and which cause hesitation. Over time, your sales process evolves automatically. Instead of training manually for months, you gain instant feedback that turns every mistake into a micro-lesson.

Another rule of the AI era is **automation doesn't mean impersonality**. Many fear that automated systems make interactions robotic. The truth is the opposite—AI can actually make sales more human by freeing you from repetitive tasks. When automation handles data entry, scheduling, and follow-ups, you have more time to connect personally with qualified leads. Imagine having an AI assistant that automatically updates your CRM, sends polite reminders, tracks engagement, and drafts proposals while you focus on closing deals. Instead of working harder, you work smarter, supported by technology that amplifies your human strengths—empathy, creativity, and persuasion.

As sales cycles accelerate, **timing becomes more valuable than talent**. With AI, timing is no longer a lucky guess—it's a measurable metric. Predictive analytics tools monitor signals such as when a lead opens your email, downloads your brochure, or visits your pricing page. They alert you in real time when interest peaks. This allows you to strike precisely when curiosity turns into intent. In sales, seconds can make the difference between a win and a lost opportunity. AI ensures those seconds always work in your favor. Furthermore, AI is revolutionizing the **psychology of**

selling. Human buyers are emotional, not logical. They buy based on trust, urgency, and resonance. Sentiment analysis—an AI feature that interprets emotional tone in messages—helps you adapt your responses dynamically. If a prospect's tone shifts from interest to hesitation, the system can recommend empathy-based language to rebuild confidence. This technology doesn't remove humanity—it enhances it, giving you real-time emotional intelligence that was once impossible to scale.

These new rules redefine the salesperson's identity. You're no longer just a persuader—you're a strategist, a data analyst, and a relationship architect. Your success depends on your ability to orchestrate automation tools, interpret insights, and design journeys that feel seamless. You become the human conductor of a symphony of intelligent systems, ensuring every note—every email, call, and conversation—resonates with precision.

Finally, the biggest shift is **from chasing to attracting**. The traditional salesperson hunts for leads. The modern AI-powered seller builds digital ecosystems that attract and convert them automatically. AI-driven content recommendations, chatbots on your website, and automated lead magnets create a pipeline that never sleeps. When a visitor engages with your chatbot, the system identifies their intent, scores their interest, and begins nurturing them with relevant follow-ups. By the time you step in, the prospect already trusts your brand and sees you as the logical solution.

In the chapters ahead, we'll go deeper into each of these principles—how to set up your AI lead generation systems, automate nurturing, integrate CRMs with AI assistants, and use predictive analytics to close deals faster. But remember, every revolution begins with understanding. The new rules of selling don't erase the old—they refine them. Selling will always be about people, problems, and solutions. AI just gives you a faster, smarter, and more powerful way to connect those dots. The more you embrace it, the more unstoppable your growth will become.

"The One-Person Sales Team"

Daniel Ruiz sat in front of his laptop at 2:14 a.m., staring at an empty CRM. He had spent the last six months trying to rebuild his freelance consulting business after losing his biggest client. Cold calls, LinkedIn messages, networking events—nothing worked. He wasn't lazy; he was exhausted. Every day felt like shouting into the void. Then one night, while scrolling through YouTube, he stumbled upon a video titled *"How I Automated My Entire Sales Process With AI."* At first, he laughed. But something about the video—its simplicity, its promise—made him curious enough to try.

The next morning, Daniel set up a free trial of Apollo.io and ChatGPT. He uploaded his client list and asked ChatGPT to write a personalized outreach email for each contact. To his surprise, the emails sounded genuine, not robotic. One read: *"Hey Mark, I saw you recently expanded your real estate firm into Tampa. Congratulations! I specialize in helping new offices cut their onboarding costs by 30%."* It felt natural, almost human. He sent it. Within hours, Mark replied: *"Let's talk."*

Encouraged, Daniel built a workflow: ChatGPT wrote the first email, Apollo scheduled the sequence, and a simple Zapier connection updated responses in his Google Sheet. He wasn't tech-savvy, but the tools were intuitive. Each night, he'd test a new idea. Within a week, he had a miniature sales engine running while he slept. When he woke up each morning, his inbox was full of replies—from leads he hadn't even contacted personally.

One night, he integrated an AI chatbot on his website. It asked visitors questions like, "What's your biggest challenge right now?" and "Would you like a free proposal?" The chatbot didn't just collect answers; it analyzed tone. When someone responded with curiosity, it flagged them as "warm." When someone expressed frustration, it sent an empathetic message: *"Sounds like you're dealing with some big challenges. Would you like a quick strategy video?"* The next morning, Daniel found two new booked calls—and one of them converted into a $4,800 contract.

Over the next few weeks, Daniel transformed from desperate to deliberate. He no longer chased leads; they found him. The AI system told him which prospects were most engaged, when to follow up, and what message to send. He began to understand something profound: AI didn't replace his salesmanship—it amplified it. The machine handled the noise; he handled the nuance. Every call felt more intentional, every deal more natural.

One afternoon, while sipping coffee on his porch, Daniel looked at his phone and saw the notification: *"Monthly revenue: $14,260."* It wasn't millions, but it was freedom. He hadn't hired anyone, yet his business operated like a team of five. The AI tools worked tirelessly—analyzing, writing, scheduling—while he focused on delivering results. The exhaustion that once haunted him was gone, replaced by excitement. He felt in control again, not of the economy or the market, but of his time.

Weeks later, during a virtual networking event, someone asked how he managed to grow so fast. Daniel smiled and said, *"I didn't hire a team. I built one with AI."* The others laughed politely, not realizing he meant it literally. His AI-powered systems had become his silent partners—ones that never asked for commission or days off.

As the sun set behind his laptop, Daniel realized that he hadn't just learned how to sell differently—he had learned how to think differently. Selling wasn't about volume anymore; it was about velocity, precision, and connection. He closed his laptop, confident that even as he slept, his new team—his invisible, intelligent allies—were still out there closing the next deal.

Chapter 2: AI Prospecting: Finding Your Perfect Leads Automatically

In traditional sales, prospecting has always been the most exhausting part of the process. It's the phase that separates amateurs from professionals—the hours spent searching for the right contact, the countless "no responses," and the endless guessing about who might actually buy. But the rise of AI has completely redefined what prospecting means. It's no longer about quantity; it's about precision. AI prospecting isn't about chasing everyone—it's about identifying *the right someone* before your competitors do.

The first shift is understanding that **data is the new salesperson**. AI-powered tools like Apollo, Clay, ZoomInfo, and LeadIQ can now crawl millions of online profiles, business directories, and engagement signals to uncover leads that fit your ideal customer profile with uncanny accuracy. Instead of manually filtering by job title or industry, AI analyzes behavior—who's recently raised funding, launched a new product, or changed leadership. These subtle shifts often indicate buying intent long before a prospect ever fills out a form. The result is a curated list of high-probability leads that actually want what you sell, even if they don't know it yet.

But the magic of AI prospecting doesn't stop at lead

discovery—it extends to **lead scoring and prioritization**. In the past, you had to trust your intuition to decide which prospect deserved your time. Now, predictive models can assign each lead a "conversion probability score." They analyze email engagement, website visits, social media activity, and CRM data to determine how likely a lead is to buy. Tools like HubSpot's AI scoring or Pipedrive's Smart Data Enrichment let you open your dashboard and instantly see which ten leads you should contact first—and which ones can wait. The result is a focused sales process where your energy goes only where it produces results.

AI also introduces **intent-based prospecting**, one of the most powerful evolutions in sales intelligence. Imagine being able to know who's actively searching for your product right now. Intent platforms like Bombora and Demandbase track anonymous web behavior across millions of domains. They identify when companies are researching specific topics—say, "AI sales automation" or "CRM integration"—and alert you immediately. That's your moment to strike. Instead of cold outreach, you're entering a warm conversation, positioning yourself as the right solution at the right time.

Another advantage is **prospect enrichment**. AI can transform a basic name and email into a complete buyer profile. Using natural language models, it can summarize a person's job history, communication style, interests, and even predict how they prefer to be approached. For instance, you can ask ChatGPT: "Summarize this LinkedIn profile and write a friendly introduction message that fits this person's tone." The AI reads between the lines of posts, endorsements, and career moves—something no human could do at scale. Within seconds, you have a personalized outreach that feels handcrafted.

Once your AI systems are finding and scoring the right leads, the next step is **automation**. Instead of switching between multiple apps, you can connect your entire lead ecosystem using Make.com or Zapier. For example, you can set up a workflow that automatically imports new leads from Apollo into your CRM, scores them using OpenAI, and triggers a personalized outreach campaign. Each step happens without manual effort, yet the results feel personal. You're creating a living, breathing prospecting machine that never stops working.

AI prospecting also enhances **efficiency for solopreneurs and small businesses**. In the past, prospecting was a task that required entire teams of assistants or data researchers. Today, a single entrepreneur can achieve the same output as a corporate sales department. AI filters the noise, eliminating unqualified prospects and repetitive tasks. It becomes your digital researcher, your assistant, and your strategist—all in one. When you wake up each morning, your inbox isn't full of random names; it's filled with opportunities already analyzed and prioritized for you.

But to unlock the full potential of AI prospecting, you need to treat it as a partnership, not a shortcut. The tools can deliver data, but *you* bring the insight. Your role is to interpret, refine, and feed the system with context—what worked, what didn't, and what types of clients bring the highest lifetime value. Over time, your AI learns from your feedback and becomes sharper. Every click, call, and closed deal teaches the system how to find more people like your best customers.

Finally, remember that AI prospecting is not just about finding leads—it's about **creating alignment between technology and empathy**. The goal isn't to automate outreach to the point of impersonality; it's to use automation to understand people better. When your AI suggests that a prospect is struggling with slow response times or outdated systems, it's your chance to lead with value, not volume. Use those insights to open conversations that feel genuine and relevant.

The future of sales will belong to those who balance automation with authenticity. The tools will only get smarter, faster, and more predictive. Your job is to ensure they remain human-centered. When AI finds your perfect leads automatically, it doesn't just save you time—it gives you something far more valuable: the freedom to focus on what you do best—building relationships, solving problems, and closing deals with confidence.

"The Night the Leads Found Him"

Two weeks after automating his first outreach, Daniel Ruiz realized something incredible—his small system was working, but he wanted more control. He was tired of chasing cold leads, hoping someone would respond. He wanted the kind of prospects who were already thinking about hiring someone like him. So one evening, while sipping coffee in his apartment, he decided to take AI prospecting to the next level.

He started by signing up for a new tool he'd heard about—Clay. It claimed to build hyper-targeted lead lists using AI filters. Daniel entered a few prompts: *"Find small business owners in real estate or finance who recently posted about hiring or automation."* Within minutes, the tool generated hundreds of results. But instead of just names, it provided insights: who was hiring, who had just received funding, who recently mentioned sales automation on LinkedIn. Each detail felt like a clue, and Daniel began to realize what salespeople meant when they said, *"data is gold."*

He then connected Clay to his CRM through Make.com. The leads flowed in automatically, complete with context—company size, recent activity, even the tone of their latest post. Daniel customized ChatGPT to analyze each profile and create a personal note. One message read: *"Hi Sarah, I saw you mentioned hiring help for your real estate marketing team. I specialize in automation that reduces lead costs by 40%—would you be open to a short strategy chat?"* He hit send. Within an hour, she replied: *"Yes, I've been trying to figure that out. Let's connect tomorrow."*

For the first time, Daniel didn't feel like he was fishing in an empty pond. He felt like the fish were swimming to him. As days passed, his AI system began to *learn*. It noticed which industries replied faster, which keywords generated better engagement, and even what subject lines boosted open rates. He didn't have to think about it—the system adapted automatically. It was like having a junior sales team silently studying every move he made.

Late one night, as rain tapped against the window, Daniel received an alert: *"New lead intent detected: 'AI sales automation'—Miami, Florida."* He clicked. The company was a mid-sized marketing agency looking to streamline their client acquisition. The intent data showed they had recently downloaded multiple guides about automation and AI tools.

Daniel smiled—he didn't even have to guess. These were the perfect clients. He sent a message, customized in tone and timing, and within twenty-four hours, they were on a video call.

The conversation flowed effortlessly. Daniel no longer needed to push or persuade. The AI had already done the heavy lifting—identifying interest, qualifying leads, and preparing the path. All he had to do was show up and deliver value. By the end of the week, he had closed two new clients and booked another five consultations. He looked at his calendar and laughed softly. Six months ago, he couldn't find a single lead. Now, they were finding him.

The system ran quietly, 24/7, connecting dots he couldn't even see. When he checked his dashboard, it showed activity heatmaps, sentiment trends, and real-time engagement rates. It was like watching his business breathe—alive, intelligent, and self-improving. But what amazed him most wasn't the technology; it was how human it still felt. The messages were warm, the timing perfect, and every conversation began with relevance instead of awkward introduction.

One night, as he reviewed his progress, Daniel thought back to something he'd once read: *"You can't automate authenticity."* He finally understood. AI could find people, filter data, and craft the perfect message—but it was still his honesty and enthusiasm that closed the deal. Technology had given him leverage, but humanity gave him purpose. The perfect combination.

Daniel turned off the lights and left his desk, knowing the system would keep working through the night. Somewhere, a future client was typing a LinkedIn post, and his AI would notice it, analyze it, and prepare a thoughtful reply before morning. He smiled. The hunt was over. The future had flipped the script—*he no longer found leads; leads found him.*

Chapter 3: AI Outreach: Writing Messages That Get Replies Using ChatGPT and Automation

If AI prospecting is the art of finding the right people, AI outreach is the science of starting the right conversation. In sales, it's not enough to have leads—you need engagement. You can have the most qualified prospects in the world, but if your messages don't connect, your pipeline stays dry. Traditional outreach often fails because it's generic. People can feel when they're just another name in a list. The new era of selling demands something different—messages that sound personal, relevant, and timely. That's exactly where AI, particularly natural language tools like ChatGPT, becomes your most valuable sales partner.

At its core, AI outreach uses data and personalization models to create hyper-specific communication that resonates with the receiver. Every great sales message has three invisible ingredients: context, empathy, and clarity. Context means you understand who the person is and what they care about. Empathy means you speak their language and mirror their mindset. Clarity means you state your value quickly, without jargon or fluff. AI can now weave these elements into every message you send. With the right prompt, ChatGPT can analyze a prospect's social media, website, and tone to generate a message that feels written by someone who truly understands their needs.

The key is to **train your AI to think like a trusted advisor, not a marketer**. For example, instead of saying, *"Hey John, I help companies like yours automate sales processes,"* you can instruct ChatGPT to write: *"Hi John, I noticed your team just launched a new marketing campaign—congrats! If part of your focus this quarter is streamlining follow-ups or lead tracking, I'd love to share a quick workflow that's been working for others in your industry."* It's specific, conversational, and respectful. The difference is not in the words—it's in the psychology. AI helps you capture that subtle tone that opens doors instead of closing them.

Another powerful aspect of AI outreach is **sequencing**. Sales outreach is rarely one message—it's a process. AI tools like Smartlead, Instantly, or Lemlist can combine ChatGPT-written messages with automated follow-ups that adapt to responses. For instance, if a lead opens an email but doesn't reply, the AI can send a softer, value-driven follow-up three days later. If they click a link or engage with your site, it can trigger a calendar invite or personalized case study. Each step feels human but runs entirely on autopilot. The secret is to feed the

AI context at every step—what tone to use, what objections to anticipate, what value to emphasize.

You can also use **AI-powered split testing** to continuously improve your messaging. Instead of guessing which outreach style works best, you can run dozens of variations simultaneously. ChatGPT can help you generate multiple subject lines or message formats—friendly, professional, urgent, storytelling—and your automation system can measure which versions perform best. Over time, the AI learns your audience's emotional language. It identifies which words trigger curiosity, which phrases build trust, and which call-to-actions convert most effectively. That's not just automation—that's persuasion at scale.

However, the most effective AI outreach still follows a timeless truth: people buy from people they trust. That's why every message should aim to *start a conversation, not close a sale.* Use your first touchpoint to ask thoughtful questions or offer genuine insights. For example, instead of pushing for a call immediately, try something like: *"Would it be helpful if I shared the 3-step workflow I use to cut response time by half?"* It feels collaborative, not pushy. AI can generate dozens of these micro-invitations that lower resistance and open real dialogue.

To maximize success, integrate your AI outreach with **CRM automation**. When a prospect replies, AI can categorize the tone (positive, neutral, or negative), suggest next steps, and even draft your follow-up reply. You become a strategist rather than a typist. You log in to your system and see a dashboard full of pre-drafted responses waiting for your final touch. It's like having an assistant who writes, thinks, and adapts on your behalf.

Remember that personalization doesn't mean perfection—it means relevance. You don't need a message that sounds flawless; you need one that feels real. AI excels at scaling that "human touch." When you feed it insights like your target's industry, challenges, or language style, it can create messages that mirror human understanding. A well-trained AI will never send a robotic, lifeless note—it will sound like *you on your best day*.

The final layer of AI outreach is **emotional timing**. Every lead moves through an invisible cycle of curiosity, interest, and readiness. AI helps you detect that rhythm. It tracks when emails are opened, when links are clicked, and when replies are delayed. It can adjust the outreach sequence automatically, maintaining engagement without overstepping. It's no longer a guessing game—it's a dance choreographed by data.

In this new age, the most successful sellers are not the loudest they're the most relevant. AI doesn't just make your outreach faster; it makes it meaningful. It allows you to show empathy at scale, precision at speed, and professionalism without friction. When you master AI outreach, you stop being another salesperson in someone's inbox—you become a voice they want to hear again.

"The Message That Changed Everything"

The morning sun spilled through Daniel Ruiz's apartment window as his phone buzzed with notifications. His AI prospecting system had pulled in forty-seven new leads overnight. But today wasn't about finding new names—it was about connecting. Daniel had built his foundation; now it was time to turn interest into opportunity. He opened his email platform, where ChatGPT had generated dozens of new outreach messages overnight.

He clicked the first one, addressed to a marketing director named Allison. It read: *"Hi Allison, I loved your recent post on how client communication builds loyalty. I've been helping agencies like yours automate personalized follow-ups without losing that human tone you value so much. Would you be open to seeing how I do it?"* Daniel smiled. It didn't sound like an ad. It sounded like a conversation. He approved it, and within minutes, his automation system queued it up for delivery.

Hours later, as he reviewed analytics, one notification stood out—Allison had opened the email three times and clicked the link twice. The AI flagged it as a high-intent lead and automatically sent a follow-up: *"Just wanted to check if tomorrow or Thursday works better for a quick chat?"* Ten minutes later, she replied: *"Tomorrow's perfect. This is exactly what I've been looking for."*

Daniel leaned back in his chair, amazed. Weeks ago, he'd been writing messages manually, trying to sound professional but often coming across stiff or generic. Now, every email he sent felt alive—with warmth, curiosity, and precision. The AI wasn't replacing him—it was amplifying his best instincts.

Over the next few days, his inbox filled with replies. Some said "not now," others said "maybe later," but more and more said "yes." Each interaction refined the system. When someone didn't reply, the AI waited patiently, then sent a subtle nudge. When someone showed hesitation, it analyzed tone and crafted reassurance. It was like having a sales assistant with emotional intelligence.

One evening, Daniel decided to test a new workflow. He uploaded a short video introduction of himself explaining what he did, and asked ChatGPT to write a personal message that included it. The AI crafted something simple: *"Hi Michael, I recorded a short 60-second video to show how small businesses are using AI to close deals faster—no pressure, just sharing something that's been helpful."* The next morning, three of his prospects had watched the video. One wrote back: *"I'm impressed by how human this feels. Let's talk."*

As weeks passed, Daniel's reputation began to spread. Clients weren't just buying his services—they were asking how he managed to follow up so naturally. They couldn't believe he was doing it all himself. He'd smile and say, *"I have a great system."* But the truth was, the system had become his silent partner—predicting, personalizing, and performing at a level he never thought possible.

Then came the email that changed everything. It was from a large consulting firm. They'd been quietly observing his outreach for weeks. The message read: *"Your approach is the most refreshing we've seen in a long time. Would you be open to running an AI outreach campaign for our team?"* Daniel reread the email twice, heart racing. He had gone from struggling freelancer to consultant for consultants.

That night, as he closed his laptop, he thought about how far he'd come. AI had taught him that selling wasn't about chasing—it was about connecting. Each message was no longer a pitch; it was a bridge. The future of sales wasn't mechanical—it was musical. AI had simply tuned the instrument.

He looked out the window at the city lights and whispered to himself, *"I didn't just build a system. I built a voice."* And that voice, powered by AI but grounded in authenticity, was now being heard by the world.

Chapter 4: AI Follow-Up Mastery: Nurturing Leads Until They're Ready to Buy

The fortune is—and always has been—in the follow-up. In sales, success doesn't come from the first contact but from the consistent, intelligent, and timely communication that follows. Studies show that nearly 80% of sales happen after the fifth contact, yet most sellers give up after one or two. The reason? Follow-up fatigue. It's exhausting to remember who to message, when to reach out again, and what to say next. But this is where artificial intelligence turns repetition into rhythm. With the right AI systems, following up is no longer manual—it's automatic, personalized, and perfectly timed.

AI follow-up mastery begins with understanding **buyer readiness cycles**. Not every lead is ready to buy immediately. Some are curious, others cautious, and a few are actively comparing options. In the past, managing this required intuition and spreadsheets. Today, AI can analyze behavioral signals—email opens, website visits, content engagement—and automatically classify leads by intent level. When a prospect starts re-engaging with your emails or visiting your pricing page, the AI flags it and triggers a message tailored to that stage. It doesn't just send reminders—it nurtures relationships.

The goal is not to chase people but to **stay relevant in their awareness** until the timing is right. That's where AI-driven nurturing sequences come in. Tools like ActiveCampaign, HubSpot, and Instantly integrate with ChatGPT to craft multi-step email journeys that adapt dynamically. For example, if a prospect opens your email but doesn't reply, the AI can send a helpful guide related to their industry three days later. If they click that guide, it follows up with a short testimonial or video. If they remain inactive, the tone shifts—light, friendly check-ins that maintain connection without pressure. Each action triggers the next best step automatically, turning follow-up into an intelligent conversation flow.

The most powerful part of this process is **adaptive tone modeling**. AI can now adjust your follow-up language based on emotional cues. Sentiment analysis tools read replies for enthusiasm, hesitation, or resistance. If a prospect sounds uncertain, the AI can recommend empathy-driven responses: "No worries, I completely understand your timing. I'll send over a few resources that might help when you're ready." These micro-adjustments maintain trust while keeping the relationship alive. It's emotional intelligence at scale—something no manual system can replicate consistently.

Consistency is another key pillar. Human follow-up often fails because it's inconsistent. We get busy, distracted, or discouraged. AI never does. It remembers every lead, every response, every date. It sends the perfect message at the perfect time, even months later. Imagine your AI system automatically checking in with a prospect ninety days after your first conversation—reminding them of your value, referencing past messages, and reigniting the dialogue. To the prospect, it feels thoughtful. To you, it's completely hands-free.

AI also revolutionizes the **content strategy behind nurturing**. Instead of sending static reminders, it can personalize educational materials for each lead. One person may receive an AI-generated case study showing how you helped a similar client. Another may get a brief voice message recorded by you, distributed automatically through an AI tool that personalizes greetings. The key principle is *value before urgency*. When your follow-ups educate, entertain, or inspire rather than pressure, your brand becomes trusted instead of forgotten.

But AI follow-up mastery isn't just about automation—it's about **timing alignment**. Every market and industry has its own rhythm. Some leads require weekly touches; others, quarterly. AI analytics can identify your optimal cadence by studying conversion patterns. It notices that prospects who received five touches over 30 days convert at double the rate of those who received three. It learns, adapts, and refines. The system becomes smarter every week, continuously fine-tuning the balance between persistence and patience.

One of the most underrated uses of AI in follow-up is **re-engagement automation**. Old leads aren't dead—they're dormant. AI can resurface past conversations, update the contact's situation via LinkedIn or news data, and craft a contextual re-entry message. Something as simple as, "I saw your company just expanded into Miami—congratulations! That's actually where I've been helping teams automate outreach lately," can reopen doors long thought closed. The system never forgets. It waits, watches, and strikes when the time is right.

At its highest level, AI follow-up mastery transforms your business into a *relationship engine*. Every interaction becomes part of a living system that learns how to build trust, not just track tasks. You stop chasing opportunities and start orchestrating them. AI gives you the structure, but your authenticity gives it soul. When those two merge, you achieve something rare: a follow-up strategy that feels both mechanical in consistency and human in warmth.

In the end, follow-up mastery is about showing you care enough to stay. AI doesn't just make that easier—it makes it inevitable. When you combine automation with empathy, you stop losing leads to neglect and start winning them through nurture. The system never sleeps, never forgets, and never misses a chance to remind someone that you're still there—ready when they are.

"The Email That Wouldn't Quit"

By now, Daniel Ruiz's business was thriving. Leads were coming in daily, and replies filled his inbox. But he noticed something interesting: not everyone who replied was ready to buy. Some said, *"We'll revisit this next quarter,"* or *"I'm not the decision-maker, but this looks interesting."* In the old days, Daniel would've let those fade away. But now, with his AI system evolving, he wondered—what if no lead ever slipped through the cracks again?

He spent the evening building a nurturing workflow. He fed ChatGPT a list of previous conversations—those that ended politely but without a deal. Then he asked, *"Write a 6-step follow-up sequence that keeps me top-of-mind for the next 90 days."* Within moments, the AI responded with a plan: light check-ins, resource-sharing messages, subtle reintroductions. It even recommended when to send each one based on engagement data. Daniel linked it to his CRM, hit activate, and watched the magic unfold.

Three days later, one of his "cold" leads, a startup founder named Jenna, received a new message: *"Hey Jenna, I just finished a new workflow that cuts response time by 40%. Thought you might find it interesting since we spoke about lead bottlenecks last month."* She replied almost immediately: *"Perfect timing—let's revisit this. Can we talk tomorrow?"* Daniel smiled. The system had done exactly what he hoped—stayed patient but persistent.

As the weeks went on, the follow-ups continued automatically. The AI tracked every open, click, and response. When someone ignored a message, it adjusted tone and frequency. When someone engaged, it elevated them to Daniel's personal follow-up list. What used to be chaos was now choreography. His sales pipeline didn't feel like a guessing game anymore—it felt alive, breathing, and intelligent.

One morning, Daniel woke up to an email from an old lead he hadn't thought about in months. *"Hey, I've been meaning to reach back out. I loved those tips you sent—let's get something started."* The timestamp? Exactly ninety-one days since their first conversation. His AI had sent a friendly check-in the day before. Timing that perfect couldn't be coincidence—it was design.

But it wasn't just about automation; it was about emotion. Daniel began adding personal touches to the sequences—a quick selfie video saying thanks, a short note signed with his name. The AI distributed them automatically, customizing each greeting. People started replying not just to do business, but to say, *"I appreciate your consistency. You actually stayed in touch when no one else did."*

Then came his biggest breakthrough. One of his earliest prospects—a regional agency that had gone silent for months—finally replied to an AI follow-up. *"We just got funding and we're ready to move forward. Can you send a proposal?"* That single message turned into a $12,000 contract. Daniel laughed aloud. His system had waited patiently for months and struck when the time was right.

Later that night, he reflected on what he'd built. His AI wasn't just sending messages—it was sustaining relationships. It remembered birthdays, anniversaries, and company milestones. It sent congratulations when clients got promoted and sympathy when they posted about challenges. What began as a machine had become something closer to a memory—a digital version of Daniel's best self, always attentive, always caring.

He realized then that follow-up wasn't about persistence. It was about presence. Staying visible. Staying valuable. Staying human—even when the communication was automated. Daniel shut his laptop, knowing his AI assistant was still working quietly behind the scenes. Somewhere out there, another lead was being reminded that he cared. And when they were finally ready, he'd be the first person they thought of.

Chapter 5: AI Pipeline Optimization: Turning Prospects Into Predictable Revenue

Every successful business eventually realizes that consistency beats excitement. A few big deals might look impressive, but what truly builds freedom is predictability—knowing with confidence what revenue is coming in each week, each month, and each quarter. That level of stability was once reserved for large corporations with massive sales departments and complex CRMs. But with artificial intelligence, even a one-person business can create a pipeline as intelligent, efficient, and data-driven as any enterprise. AI pipeline optimization is the process of turning scattered leads into a synchronized system—where every opportunity is tracked, scored, and advanced automatically toward conversion.

The foundation of AI pipeline optimization is **visibility**. You can't improve what you can't see. Traditional CRMs often overwhelm users with cluttered dashboards and manual data entry. AI eliminates that chaos by interpreting and organizing information automatically. It analyzes every interaction—emails, calls, website clicks, meeting notes—and updates lead stages in real time. Instead of spending hours updating spreadsheets, you can simply open your dashboard and see which deals are hot, which are stalled, and which need nurturing. AI-powered CRMs like HubSpot, Pipedrive, and Close.com now act like living systems that constantly audit themselves.

Next comes **lead scoring and prioritization**—the secret to focusing your energy where it matters most. AI uses historical patterns to assign probability scores to each opportunity. It studies how similar prospects behaved in the past—how many interactions occurred before they bought, what industries converted fastest, and what engagement patterns led to success. With this knowledge, your CRM evolves from being a database into a decision engine. It tells you, "These five prospects are most likely to close this week. Call them first." It's the digital equivalent of having a sales analyst whispering in your ear all day.

Pipeline optimization also means eliminating bottlenecks. In traditional systems, deals often get stuck between stages—qualified leads that never get proposals, or warm prospects that go cold waiting for follow-ups. AI can detect these weak points automatically. If it notices that leads often stall after the second meeting, it flags the pattern and suggests solutions—maybe faster response times, better proposal automation, or more persuasive content. Some CRMs even simulate "what-if" scenarios, predicting how revenue would change if conversion rates improved by specific percentages. You stop guessing and start managing based on data.

Another key layer is **forecasting**. Predictive AI uses real-time data to forecast future revenue with astonishing accuracy. It doesn't just count deals—it calculates momentum. By analyzing engagement velocity, response times, and historical conversion patterns, it can estimate not only how much revenue you'll close but *when*. You can plan your marketing, budget, and hiring decisions with clarity. What once required data scientists can now be achieved with an intuitive interface and the right automation setup.

But pipeline optimization isn't purely analytical—it's behavioral. AI can monitor communication habits and recommend improvements. For instance, it might detect that deals progress faster when you reply within two hours, or that messages sent on Tuesdays at noon convert 20% better than those sent on Fridays. This feedback loop transforms your habits into measurable assets. It teaches you how to sell not harder, but smarter—by aligning your actions with proven data trends.

The next step is **automation of stage transitions**. Instead of manually dragging leads across a pipeline board, AI does it for you. When a prospect signs a proposal, the system moves them automatically from "Negotiation" to "Closed Won." When a deal goes silent for too long, it shifts back to "Follow-Up Required" and triggers a re-engagement sequence. Each movement generates an intelligent task or message, ensuring that nothing—and no one—falls through the cracks.

The beauty of AI pipeline optimization is scalability. Whether you handle ten leads or ten thousand, the structure remains solid. AI ensures that every stage—from initial outreach to payment confirmation—is measurable, automated, and repeatable. Over time, your pipeline becomes not just a tracker, but a teacher. It shows you what's working, what's not, and where your next opportunity lies. The chaos of unpredictable income gives way to a calm sense of rhythm—a consistent flow of leads, conversions, and cash flow.

At the highest level, AI pipeline optimization transforms sales into a system of **predictable momentum**. Every deal advances based on logic, not luck. Every month ends with accuracy, not anxiety. It's no longer about chasing numbers—it's about managing energy. The tools do the heavy lifting, while you focus on relationships and creativity. This is where the dream of effortless income becomes reality—not because it's easy, but because it's intelligently engineered.

With AI as your co-pilot, your sales pipeline stops being a

collection of random names and becomes a living, breathing map of your business future. And once you master that, you'll never return to guesswork again.

"The Machine That Predicted His Future"

Daniel Ruiz had built something remarkable. His AI systems now found leads, wrote messages, and nurtured relationships automatically. But despite his success, he still faced one problem—uncertainty. Some months brought record income; others felt like droughts. The highs were thrilling, but the unpredictability kept him anxious. He wanted stability—a system that could not only sell but forecast. That's when he discovered the true power of pipeline optimization.

It started one quiet evening. He was reviewing his CRM when a small notification popped up: *"Pipeline intelligence module available—activate?"* Curious, Daniel clicked. The module promised real-time scoring, deal forecasting, and automated movement tracking. Within minutes, it connected to his emails, calendar, and proposal platform. By the next morning, his dashboard looked completely different. Instead of a messy list of names, he saw clear stages: New Leads, Engaged, Qualified, Negotiation, Closed. Each card had a score beside it—78%, 63%, 91%. The system was ranking his deals.

He opened the first one—a potential contract with a design

agency. The AI displayed a note: *"High engagement detected: multiple email opens, positive sentiment, last reply 24 hours ago. Recommended action: send proposal before 5 p.m."* Daniel followed the advice. The next day, the deal closed. He stared at the screen in disbelief. It wasn't luck—it was precision.

Over the following weeks, Daniel began to trust the system. It reminded him when leads were cooling off, suggested best times to reconnect, and even estimated monthly revenue. For the first time in his career, he could see his future—not as hope, but as numbers. The AI forecasted his income three months ahead, updating daily. Every small action—an email sent, a meeting booked, a proposal signed—adjusted the projection. It was like watching a digital crystal ball that learned from reality in real time.

But the true breakthrough came when the system detected a bottleneck. One afternoon, it flashed a red alert: *"Deals in Stage 3 (Negotiation) remain idle for an average of 12 days. Conversion probability decreasing 40%."* Daniel realized he'd been slow sending contracts. The AI suggested automating proposal delivery immediately after a verbal yes. He connected it to his document platform and tested it. Within a week, his close rate jumped by 30%.

Soon, Daniel's business ran with surgical precision. He woke each morning to a dashboard summary: which leads to call, which deals were likely to close, and what revenue to expect. He stopped guessing. His anxiety faded, replaced by confidence. The machine wasn't replacing him—it was empowering him to make smarter decisions faster.

One day, over coffee, a fellow entrepreneur asked him, "How do you manage all this alone?" Daniel smiled and turned his laptop toward him. The screen showed his pipeline in motion—deals shifting, numbers updating, forecasts recalculating. "I don't manage it," he said. "It manages me."

Later that night, he sat on his balcony, reflecting on how far he'd come. He no longer worked *inside* his business; he worked *above* it. His AI pipeline had become a silent partner—a strategist, analyst, and assistant rolled into one. The chaos of uncertainty had been replaced by clarity. The fear of slow months had disappeared, replaced by predictability.

As he watched the city lights flicker, his dashboard pinged softly: *"Projected monthly revenue: $22,450—confidence level 94%."* He smiled, knowing it wasn't magic—it was mastery. The future wasn't random anymore. It was automated, optimized, and measurable. Daniel closed his laptop and whispered to himself, *"This is what freedom feels like."*

Chapter 6: AI Closing Techniques – How to Use Automation, Data, and Empathy to Seal the Deal

Closing is the moment every sales process leads to—the instant when trust becomes transaction. In the traditional world of selling, closing was often associated with pressure: the scripted questions, the rehearsed urgency, the "what will it take to get you started today?" mindset. But in the age of artificial intelligence, closing is no longer about coercion; it's about **alignment**. When data, timing, and emotion converge, a deal closes almost effortlessly. AI has redefined the art of closing by removing guesswork, amplifying empathy, and delivering exactly what a prospect needs at the right moment.

The first principle of AI-powered closing is **knowing when a lead is ready**. In the past, you relied on instinct—a tone in an email or a hunch from a conversation. Now, predictive models can measure readiness with remarkable precision. AI analyzes signals such as open frequency, dwell time on proposals, response patterns, and even emotional tone in replies. A prospect who lingers on a pricing page, reads multiple case studies, and asks timing questions is statistically primed to buy. Your system can flag that readiness automatically and suggest the next best action: schedule a call, send a proposal, or offer a small incentive. Closing becomes a science of timing rather than tension.

Another crucial advancement is **AI-assisted proposal automation**. Tools like Qwilr, PandaDoc, or Notion-based templates integrated with GPT models can generate dynamic proposals tailored to each client's exact needs. The AI pulls data from your CRM—industry, goals, pain points—and constructs a document that feels handcrafted. It can even adjust tone and visuals based on sentiment data: formal for corporate buyers, friendly for small teams, inspirational for creative clients. When combined with e-signature automation, a deal can move from "decision" to "signed" in minutes instead of days.

But the magic of closing still lies in emotion. That's why the second pillar of AI-enhanced closing is **empathetic mirroring**. Machine-learning algorithms trained on conversation transcripts can now suggest emotionally intelligent language in real time. During video calls, tools like Gong or Fireflies can analyze tone and word choice, subtly prompting you to slow down, ask open questions, or emphasize a point of reassurance. When a prospect expresses doubt, the AI might suggest: "Acknowledge the concern before providing data." This blend of human warmth and data-backed empathy transforms the closing experience from a negotiation into a partnership.

The third principle is **micro-commitment sequencing**—a strategy AI executes flawlessly. Instead of pushing for a large "yes" all at once, AI systems help you secure a series of smaller affirmations. They send short confirmations, optional upgrades, or trial invitations that move the prospect closer to comfort. Chatbots and automated follow-ups can phrase these steps naturally: "Would you like me to reserve your slot?" or "Would it help if I walked you through onboarding?" These micro-moments reduce friction and build momentum until the final signature feels inevitable.

AI also enhances **objection handling**, one of the hardest aspects of closing. With access to thousands of successful transcript patterns, AI can recommend responses to common concerns. If a client hesitates about price, the system can instantly generate alternatives—payment plans, value breakdowns, ROI calculators—supported by proof. The responses arrive faster than hesitation can grow. By addressing resistance with calm precision, you maintain authority without pressure.

One overlooked but transformative aspect of AI closing is **data-driven empathy**—using insights not to manipulate but to understand. AI can surface context about a decision-maker's past intcractions, company milestones, or even preferred communication style. A simple note like, "Their team recently expanded—emphasize scalability," turns a generic conversation into a personal consultation. The prospect feels seen, not sold.

Finally, true mastery of AI-assisted closing comes from **seamless handoff and post-close automation**. The moment a deal is signed, AI tools trigger onboarding sequences, payment confirmations, and personalized thank-you notes. This continuation reinforces trust and sets the stage for referrals. In essence, AI doesn't just help you close—it ensures the client feels confident afterward, turning one sale into many.

Closing in the AI era is an elegant choreography between data and heart. Automation prepares the stage, analytics direct the timing, and empathy delivers the final touch. When all three align, closing no longer feels like a finish line—it feels like a handshake to begin a long-term relationship.

"The Deal That Closed Itself"

The steady hum of Daniel Ruiz's laptop filled his apartment as twilight settled over the city. His dashboard glowed with color-coded deals, most already in late negotiation. Yet one name stood out—a marketing firm in Austin that had gone quiet for a week after receiving his proposal. Old habits would have left him anxious, refreshing emails every hour. But tonight he trusted the system. At 8:14 p.m., a notification appeared: *"Prospect activity detected – proposal opened for 6 minutes, scroll depth 100%, confidence score 94%."* A second later, another message: *"Recommended action: Send short empathetic check-in."* Daniel smiled. He clicked "approve," and within seconds an email drafted by ChatGPT went out: *"Hey Lauren, I just wanted to check if everything looked good on the proposal. I can adjust anything that helps your team make the decision easier."*

Ten minutes later came the reply: *"Appreciate the follow-up! We're almost ready—could you extend the discount until Friday?"* Daniel typed back, "Yes, of course." Before he could even hit send, the AI whispered a suggestion on his screen: *"Offer to add one extra training session as a bonus instead of discount."* He revised his message, sent it, and within minutes Lauren replied: *"Deal. Let's sign tonight."*

That moment changed everything. It was the first time Daniel felt like he was co-closing with a partner that understood both numbers and nuance. He watched as the AI auto-generated the final proposal, attached the e-signature link, and sent a thank-you note the moment the document was signed. What once took days now happened in twenty minutes.

Over the next few weeks, the system became almost prophetic. It could sense buying intent before prospects expressed it. When someone read three emails in a row or downloaded two guides, it sent Daniel an alert: *"Engagement spike detected—prepare to close."* He would reach out casually, often finding the client ready to buy. The machine was reading patterns in behavior that humans would miss, and each interaction refined its intuition.

Yet for all the automation, Daniel never let go of authenticity. Before every final meeting, he recorded a personal video message thanking the client for their time. The AI helped schedule and send them, but the words were his. Clients replied with warm messages like, *"You're the only consultant who made this feel personal."* He realized the true power of AI wasn't in replacing human touch—it was in magnifying it.

Then came his biggest deal yet—a national agency looking for a sales automation consultant. The negotiation spanned three weeks. Data flowed through his dashboard like a heartbeat. Every pause, every question, every change in tone was captured and interpreted. On the final call, the AI overlay displayed a tiny prompt: *"Mirror their language—focus on security and partnership."* Daniel followed its cue. When the meeting ended, the agency's CEO said, "We like how you listen. Let's do this."

When the contract notification appeared minutes later, Daniel didn't jump up or shout. He just smiled. It no longer felt like winning a battle—it felt like completing a conversation that was always meant to end this way. The AI had guided him through the process like a coach who knew every move before it happened.

That night, as he walked outside beneath the streetlights, he checked his phone one last time. The dashboard displayed: *"Deal Closed — $48,000 annual retainer secured. Next step: onboarding automation initiated."* Daniel laughed softly. The deal had literally closed itself.

He realized then that closing wasn't an event—it was a continuum. AI had not made him less human; it had made him more aware, more present, more empathetic. He had learned to trust data without losing intuition, to automate tasks without automating relationships. And as he stood there watching his future update on a screen in real time, Daniel knew the truth that every modern closer must learn: in the age of AI, sales doesn't end with a signature—it begins with understanding.

Chapter 7: AI Upselling & Client Retention — Turning One Sale Into Lifelong Revenue

Most salespeople celebrate when a deal closes. The great ones celebrate when it renews. In business, the first sale simply opens the door; real wealth comes from what happens afterward. It's not acquisition—it's expansion. With artificial intelligence, retention and upselling are no longer dependent on memory or luck. AI gives you the ability to predict client needs, personalize ongoing value, and transform one-time buyers into lifetime partners. The smartest companies today aren't asking, "How do we find more clients?" They're asking, "How do we serve the ones we already have better than anyone else?"

The first principle of AI-driven retention is **relationship mapping**. Every client interaction—emails, meetings, deliverables—creates data that reveals satisfaction trends. AI systems analyze those signals to detect loyalty or risk. For example, if a client's engagement frequency drops, the system can alert you before they churn. If sentiment analysis shows increasingly positive feedback, AI recommends ideal timing for a renewal conversation or upsell offer. It's like having an emotional radar that spots subtle shifts before they become visible.

The second key is **personalized value reinforcement**. Traditional follow-ups often sound generic: "Just checking in" or "How are things going?" AI replaces those with contextual communication that reminds clients why they chose you in the first place. By analyzing performance data, usage metrics, or project outcomes, it can automatically craft updates like: "Since implementing your automation workflow, your response time has improved 43%. I'd love to explore extending this to your customer success team." This transforms every message into both a service and a subtle upsell.

AI also enables **predictive upselling**, where data anticipates client needs before they ask. Recommendation engines—once exclusive to e-commerce giants—are now accessible to freelancers and small businesses. By studying behavioral patterns, AI identifies complementary products or services most relevant to each customer. For example, if a client used your AI sales automation for lead generation, the system may suggest adding an onboarding automation module. These intelligent recommendations feel helpful rather than promotional because they're based on genuine relevance.

The heart of retention, however, is **consistent engagement**. AI automates the rhythm of communication without making it robotic. You can build workflows that send educational tips, milestone congratulations, and personalized updates at the perfect intervals. Every message reinforces connection. When clients feel seen, they stay. Tools like Customer.io, HubSpot, or even custom GPT workflows can manage dozens of relationships simultaneously while keeping every note warm and authentic.

Another powerful strategy is **AI-enhanced customer feedback loops**. Collecting feedback used to require surveys that few people completed. Now, natural-language processing allows AI to extract insights from conversations, emails, and reviews automatically. It summarizes praise and pain points, then recommends improvements or potential upsells aligned with what clients value most. You no longer guess what your market wants—the data tells you precisely.

Retention also thrives on **proactive problem solving**. AI doesn't just react; it predicts. Suppose a client's automation system slows down or a campaign underperforms. AI monitoring tools can flag the issue, diagnose likely causes, and even draft an outreach message offering help before the client complains. That level of foresight builds trust faster than any pitch. Clients begin to see you not as a vendor but as a partner who always shows up at the right time. Finally, true upselling mastery comes from **timing and transparency**. The best upsells are not surprises—they're logical progressions. AI helps you identify the perfect moment when satisfaction and curiosity intersect. When the system detects a client has achieved strong results, it triggers a conversation prompt like: "You've outgrown your current workflow—here's the next step to scale." Because the message is based on success, not pressure, the client sees it as guidance rather than salesmanship.

When combined, these systems form a virtuous cycle: data informs insight, insight drives engagement, engagement drives loyalty, and loyalty fuels growth. The beauty of AI retention is that it compounds over time. Each interaction adds intelligence, making your system smarter and your relationships deeper. What begins as automation evolves into genuine connection—a network of satisfied clients who not only stay but refer others.

In the AI era, closing the deal isn't the end of the journey—it's the beginning of a lifelong dialogue. Your tools can analyze, communicate, and predict, but it's your integrity and care that transform automation into allegiance. When technology amplifies service instead of replacing it, every sale becomes the seed of many more.

"The Client Who Never Left"

A month after landing his biggest contract, Daniel Ruiz noticed something unusual. Instead of chasing new leads, his dashboard kept flashing alerts from existing clients: *"Engagement drop detected," "Positive feedback spike—potential upsell opportunity."* His AI system had evolved again, this time from hunter to guardian. It wasn't just helping him close deals—it was helping him keep them.

One alert came from a long-time client, a real-estate agency he'd automated months earlier. The AI flagged: *"Activity reduced 60% over last 10 days—possible churn risk."* Daniel opened the conversation log. The emails had slowed, and the last message hinted they were "trying new tools." Normally, that would have gone unnoticed until it was too late. But now he had foresight. He typed a quick note the AI suggested: *"Hey Kevin, I saw you've been testing new automation. Just wanted to check if you'd like me to optimize your campaign results before you switch—it might save your team time."* Kevin replied within hours: *"Actually yes, we were struggling with setup—can we meet tomorrow?"* A potential loss had turned into renewal.

Encouraged, Daniel explored the other alerts. One read: *"Positive sentiment detected: client achieved milestone—ideal upsell timing."* It referred to Jenna, the startup founder he'd re-engaged months earlier. The AI had detected her posts celebrating higher lead conversions. Daniel crafted a message: *"Congrats on hitting 5,000 leads this month! Many clients at that stage scale faster by automating their follow-ups. Want me to show you how?"* She responded immediately: *"Yes, let's expand our plan."* The upsell was effortless because it was relevant.

Soon, Daniel's mornings became a ritual of reviewing insights rather than chasing prospects. His system displayed a loyalty dashboard showing satisfaction scores, engagement streaks, and lifetime value projections. When a client hit a new threshold, it triggered personalized videos, thank-you notes, or small bonuses. Clients began calling him instead of the other way around. The phrase "We're thinking of leaving" disappeared from his inbox entirely.

One evening, while reviewing analytics, the AI sent a new kind of message: *"Predictive referral opportunity: Client 'Allison' shared positive sentiment publicly."* Curious, Daniel checked LinkedIn. She had posted about his work, praising his "AI wizardry." Without prompting, she had already become his advocate. The system automatically sent her a thank-you email and a referral link offering a discount for anyone she invited. Within a week, two new clients had signed up.

But the most profound moment came months later, when Daniel's earliest client—the one who'd first trusted him during his chaotic beginnings—renewed for the third time. The AI had scheduled a renewal proposal, pre-filled with updated metrics showing 120% growth since their start. When Daniel joined the call, the client laughed, "You know, I was going to ask for an update next week. You beat me to it—again."

Daniel realized he wasn't just running a business anymore; he was building an ecosystem that cared for itself. His AI systems anticipated, nurtured, and celebrated his clients like an invisible team. Every time he thought about expansion, the data told him the truth: retention *was* expansion.

As night fell, Daniel leaned back and watched his dashboard cycle through client metrics—green bars, rising percentages, renewal notices. Each number represented a relationship sustained through empathy amplified by technology. What once felt like selling now felt like serving.

He smiled, closing his laptop. The AI would keep monitoring through the night, ensuring that no client ever felt forgotten. For the first time, Daniel understood what real success meant. It wasn't the rush of new deals—it was the quiet satisfaction of hearing from the same clients again and again. Not because they had to. But because they wanted to.

Chapter 8: AI Sales Analytics & Performance Tracking — How to Measure, Improve, and Scale Your Results

Data is the mirror of performance. In traditional sales, most professionals operated on instinct and memory—celebrating wins, guessing why they lost, and hoping next month would be better. But in the AI era, guessing is replaced by knowing. Sales analytics powered by artificial intelligence gives you more than numbers; it gives you truth. It reveals patterns you can't see, predicts trends before they happen, and turns everyday activities into measurable growth. When used correctly, AI analytics becomes the difference between working hard and working smart—between random success and consistent scaling.

The foundation of AI sales analytics lies in **real-time tracking**. Instead of reviewing spreadsheets at the end of the month, AI tools collect and interpret data as events happen. Every click, message, call, and email becomes a data point. Systems like HubSpot, Pipedrive Insights, and Close Analytics visualize these moments instantly—showing how many leads entered the funnel, how long they stayed in each stage, and what actions triggered conversions. AI organizes these details into living dashboards that evolve every minute. You no longer look back at history; you manage the present.

The second pillar is **pattern recognition**. Human beings can't easily detect trends across thousands of interactions, but AI thrives on it. It examines communication tone, engagement frequency, and response times across all your deals. Then it identifies what actually drives results. For example, it may reveal that emails sent between 10 a.m. and noon have a 40% higher reply rate, or that deals progress faster when you schedule follow-up calls within 24 hours of the first contact. These insights aren't abstract—they're actionable instructions for better performance.

One of the most powerful capabilities of AI analytics is **conversion path mapping**. The system learns the typical journey your clients take from first contact to close. It can show you how long, on average, each stage lasts and where prospects drop off most often. By analyzing that drop-off data, AI suggests specific improvements—tweaking outreach frequency, improving proposal delivery speed, or automating reminder messages. Instead of guessing where you lose momentum, you fix it at the root. Over time, your pipeline becomes frictionless, and your conversion rate climbs steadily.

AI analytics also introduces **performance benchmarking**,

allowing even small businesses to measure themselves like major corporations. By aggregating industry data, AI compares your numbers against market averages—response times, close rates, customer retention, and more. It tells you exactly how your business stacks up and where you can outperform competitors. You stop chasing vague goals like "get better results" and start setting quantifiable targets like "reduce average deal cycle from 21 to 14 days." This clarity breeds control.

The next layer is **predictive forecasting**, one of AI's greatest gifts to sales strategy. Predictive models process millions of data combinations—seasonality, engagement trends, deal values—to forecast revenue with stunning accuracy. The system can tell you not only what's likely to happen but what *to do* about it. For example, it might alert you: "If no new leads are added within five days, projected revenue will decline 18% next month." That's not just data—it's proactive strategy.

AI can even analyze your **communication effectiveness**. Tools like Gong, Refrain, or Fireflies study call transcripts and email threads, ranking factors like clarity, listening ratio, and confidence tone. The AI doesn't just critique—it coaches. It shows you what words build trust and what phrases weaken authority. Over time, this transforms every salesperson into their own optimized version—measured, refined, and precise.

But AI analytics isn't just about numbers—it's about *narrative.* The most successful professionals use data to tell stories: how they improved, why they grew, and where they're heading next. With AI summarization tools, you can generate weekly or monthly reports written in natural language. Instead of drowning in dashboards, you receive a story about your progress—what's improving, what's slowing down, and what to prioritize. It's like having a personal analyst translating complexity into clarity.

Finally, the true power of AI analytics lies in **scalability through insight loops**. Every decision you make feeds more data back into the system, which learns, adapts, and improves your next strategy. It becomes a compounding cycle of intelligence: action → measurement → optimization → growth. Over time, this creates exponential improvement. The small tweaks guided by AI today become the major revenue surges tomorrow.

When you fully integrate AI analytics into your business, you stop working reactively and start operating like a strategist. Every number has meaning. Every movement has purpose. And every goal becomes measurable. In this world, success isn't a mystery—it's a metric.

"The Dashboard of Truth"

By now, Daniel Ruiz's business had matured into something that felt less like a startup and more like a living organism. His AI systems handled prospecting, outreach, and follow-up seamlessly. His pipeline ran with mechanical precision. Yet something still bothered him—he didn't fully understand why some months exploded with sales while others plateaued. He wanted answers, not assumptions.

One night, while reviewing his CRM, a pop-up appeared: *"Activate AI Performance Analytics — Gain insights into conversion drivers."* Without hesitation, he clicked yes. Within seconds, charts, graphs, and heatmaps filled his screen. Every email, call, and message he'd ever sent was now being analyzed. The system began narrating insights in plain English: *"Average time between first contact and deal close: 16.3 days. Fastest conversions occur when follow-up happens within 12 hours. Decline rate increases 40% after 3 days of no reply."* Daniel stared in awe. He wasn't guessing anymore—he was learning.

Over the next few days, the dashboard became his teacher. It showed him that his most profitable clients shared common traits: mid-sized firms with teams of 5–15, decision-makers who engaged with video content, and those who responded to empathy-driven messages rather than discounts. The realization hit him—his ideal clients weren't just anyone who needed automation; they were those who valued personalization. He adjusted his targeting immediately, and the results were instant.

The system continued to uncover patterns. One morning, it flagged: *"Engagement drop in Week 3 of nurturing cycle. Recommend re-sequencing with new testimonial email."* Daniel followed the suggestion. Two days later, a lead that had gone silent reappeared, ready to close. It felt like the AI could sense the emotional rhythm of his prospects.

As months passed, Daniel's confidence grew. He no longer reacted to results—he predicted them. His dashboard forecasted revenue three months ahead, showing which deals were most likely to convert and which needed attention. The system even began to coach his communication style, analyzing video calls and offering subtle suggestions like, "Pause two seconds longer before responding to build rapport." The more he listened, the better he got.

Then came the defining moment. One evening, as rain poured outside, Daniel reviewed his analytics summary. The system displayed a line graph of his entire business history—from his first struggling month to his record-breaking quarter. The caption read: *"Revenue growth: 712% since implementing AI sales automation. Conversion efficiency: 3.4x increase."* He sat back in silence. It wasn't luck. It wasn't timing. It was clarity.

For the first time, Daniel understood what his business truly was—a collection of measurable cause and effect. Every win had a reason, every dip a solution. His AI had given him not just visibility, but mastery. He was no longer the overwhelmed freelancer guessing his way forward; he was the architect of a data-driven enterprise.

He began sharing insights with clients, using analytics to show them their own potential. They were fascinated. Many asked him to build similar systems for their teams. And so, another layer of business emerged—not just service delivery but analytics consulting. Daniel realized his data didn't just improve sales; it created new opportunities entirely.

That night, before closing his laptop, he glanced at his dashboard one last time. The AI summarized his week: *"Highest engagement this month. Forecasted revenue: $36,200. Confidence level: 96%."* He smiled. There was no anxiety, no uncertainty—only direction.

As he turned off the lights, Daniel thought back to his early days, when he'd stay up late writing cold emails that no one answered. Now, his system didn't just talk—it listened. It didn't just measure—it mentored. He understood that success wasn't hidden in mystery anymore—it was written in the numbers, waiting for those who dared to look.

Chapter 9: AI Sales Team Automation – Managing, Coaching, and Scaling with Intelligent Systems

Scaling a sales operation used to mean hiring more people, increasing costs, and losing control. But artificial intelligence has completely rewritten that equation. With the right systems in place, you can manage a growing team—or even multiple teams—without increasing complexity. AI doesn't just automate repetitive tasks; it augments human ability, creating smarter, more self-sufficient sales teams. The modern sales leader's role is no longer to micromanage but to orchestrate—using intelligent systems that guide, coach, and optimize every step of the sales process automatically.

The foundation of AI sales team automation begins with **centralized visibility**. In traditional management, information is fragmented—each salesperson keeps their own notes, schedules, and methods. AI-integrated CRMs unify it all. Every conversation, lead status, and performance metric is tracked in real time and organized into dashboards accessible to both manager and team. Tools like HubSpot Sales Hub, Salesforce Einstein, and Close.com use AI to monitor trends across the team—detecting where deals stall, who's overperforming, and what actions lead to success. Instead of guessing who needs help, you *know* instantly.

The next layer is **AI-driven task automation**, which removes administrative friction from your team's workflow. Salespeople often spend up to 60% of their time on data entry, scheduling, and reporting. AI eliminates those tasks. Calls are logged automatically, emails are categorized, follow-ups are scheduled, and notes are summarized instantly. The result: your team focuses on conversations, not clerical work. AI even prioritizes daily tasks based on deal urgency, ensuring that everyone works on what matters most.

Coaching is where AI truly shines. Old-school management relied on weekly reviews and subjective feedback. AI transforms coaching into an ongoing, objective process. Conversation analytics tools like Gong, Fireflies, and Refrain record and analyze every sales call, offering real-time insights such as talk-to-listen ratios, filler word counts, tone of voice, and emotional cues. The system identifies patterns that lead to conversions and provides personalized coaching suggestions automatically. For example, it might tell a team member, "Your close rate improves 20% when you ask two open-ended questions before presenting solutions." These micro-insights compound over time, turning every rep into a more skilled communicator.

Beyond performance, AI enables **predictive collaboration**—aligning teams around shared goals using data. By analyzing historical success patterns, the system can recommend which salesperson is best suited for a specific type of lead. It can even match clients to reps based on communication style compatibility or past conversion success. This data-driven matching boosts both morale and results, eliminating the randomness that often defines lead assignments.

Another dimension of scaling with AI is **recruitment and onboarding**. Hiring used to be a gamble, relying on resumes and gut feeling. AI changes that by analyzing candidate speech patterns, experience, and behavioral data to predict fit. Once onboarded, AI-guided training systems like Lessonly or Spekit deliver customized learning modules based on each salesperson's strengths and weaknesses. Instead of one-size-fits-all training, every rep follows a unique development path that evolves dynamically.

But the real breakthrough in AI sales management comes from **automated performance intelligence**. Instead of waiting for quarterly reports, AI tracks progress continuously—alerting you when performance metrics rise or fall. If a rep's response time increases or their sentiment in calls shifts, the system flags it early. You can then address burnout, motivation, or workload issues before they become problems. This real-time awareness creates a culture of proactive leadership rather than reactive correction.

Finally, AI transforms scaling into a predictable science. By analyzing pipeline health, conversion ratios, and workload distribution, AI can forecast exactly when to hire, what roles to fill, and how much revenue new team members will likely generate. You no longer expand based on ambition—you expand based on precision. The system ensures you grow sustainably, profitably, and strategically.

In essence, AI sales team automation doesn't replace leadership—it elevates it. It allows managers to focus on vision, culture, and human connection while AI handles the mechanics. The result is a team that moves as one cohesive, data-informed unit—efficient, consistent, and motivated by clarity. When people and machines collaborate seamlessly, scale is no longer chaotic. It becomes effortless.

"The Team That Led Itself"

Daniel Ruiz had built his empire from a laptop and late nights. But as success poured in, his inbox became overwhelming. More clients meant more projects, more calls, more follow-ups. For the first time, he realized that even automation had its limits when it was just him. It was time to grow. He hired two sales assistants—Maya and Julian—to help manage leads and client communication. But managing them manually felt like stepping back in time. He needed to find a way to lead without losing the efficiency that had built his business.

One morning, Daniel opened his CRM and noticed a new update: *"AI Team Management Mode – Monitor, Coach, and Optimize Sales Teams Automatically."* He activated it. Within minutes, the system mapped every lead across his team's activity. A color-coded dashboard appeared showing which deals were hot, which needed follow-up, and where each rep excelled. Maya's conversion rate was high with creative agencies; Julian thrived with real-estate clients. The AI highlighted patterns Daniel hadn't noticed, then suggested lead reassignment to maximize outcomes.

Soon, Daniel didn't have to tell his team what to do—the system did it for him. Every morning, Maya and Julian received personalized task lists: prioritized leads, message templates, and follow-up reminders. Calls were logged, summaries auto-written, and proposals generated with one click. Daniel spent his days reviewing insights instead of micromanaging. The AI kept everything flowing, like an invisible project manager.

The next breakthrough came with coaching. The AI analyzed their sales calls, identifying where each rep could improve. Maya's tone was engaging but sometimes rushed during pricing discussions. Julian had great rapport but didn't ask enough qualifying questions. The system didn't criticize—it coached. It sent private notes: *"Maya, pause three seconds after sharing price to let clients respond." "Julian, try asking what success looks like for them before suggesting packages."* Within weeks, both improved dramatically.

Daniel noticed something even more profound: his small team began to act like a synchronized unit. When Maya closed a deal, the system automatically assigned Julian to handle onboarding tasks. When Julian's schedule filled, the AI redistributed new leads. The entire operation adjusted dynamically, balancing workload like a living organism. Daniel didn't just have a team—he had a self-optimizing system.

One afternoon, while reviewing analytics, the AI highlighted a concern: *"Maya's average response time increased 22% this week—possible overload detected."* Daniel reached out, realizing she'd been managing too many inquiries. The system's early alert prevented burnout before it happened. The next day, it suggested redistributing leads and offering Maya a short break. For the first time, Daniel felt like his business cared for its people as much as its profits.

As the months passed, the team grew to five members, each guided by AI. Performance reports generated automatically, training modules adjusted to each person's progress, and every quarter ended with record results. Clients praised the consistency, never realizing half the coordination was handled by algorithms quietly working in the background.

But the true test came when Daniel stepped away for two weeks on vacation. He left instructions with the AI system: *"Maintain all operations, monitor metrics, and send daily summaries."* When he returned, revenue hadn't dipped—it had increased. The system had delegated tasks, optimized pipelines, and kept morale high. His team hadn't just survived—they'd thrived.

That night, as Daniel sat watching his dashboard glow, he realized something profound: he wasn't managing a team anymore. He was managing intelligence—both human and artificial. The boundaries had blurred. His people weren't threatened by automation; they were empowered by it. AI didn't make them less human—it gave them space to be *more* human: creative, empathetic, and strategic.

Daniel smiled, thinking about what lay ahead. His business could now grow infinitely without collapsing under its own weight. Leadership, he realized, wasn't about control—it was about systems that allowed people to perform at their best. And thanks to AI, his team could now lead itself.

Chapter 10: AI Sales Mastery – Building a Fully Automated, Scalable, and Human-Centered Sales Empire

Every revolution begins with a breakthrough, but mastery begins with balance. In the age of artificial intelligence, the real advantage is no longer just speed or automation—it's harmony between human intention and machine intelligence. Sales mastery means building a system that works for you, scales with you, and reflects your values. It's not about replacing people with code; it's about designing an intelligent ecosystem that multiplies your impact while keeping you grounded in authenticity. The future of sales is not purely digital—it's *augmented human.*

The foundation of AI sales mastery is **complete integration**. True automation isn't achieved through fragmented tools—it's achieved when your systems talk to each other. Imagine every part of your business—lead generation, outreach, follow-up, analytics, invoicing, and client support—connected through one intelligent infrastructure. Platforms like Make.com, Zapier, or native AI CRMs can centralize all workflows into a seamless engine. When a lead responds to your outreach, the AI updates the CRM, triggers a personalized reply, books a call, sends a reminder, and even predicts the deal's closing probability. What once took hours now happens invisibly. This level of orchestration frees your time for the only task automation cannot replicate—vision.

The next principle is **strategic delegation to machines**. Mastery doesn't mean doing everything yourself; it means designing systems that do it for you while maintaining your voice. The best sales empires are built on frameworks where AI handles 80% of the process, and humans focus on the 20% that builds trust and emotion. Lead scoring, proposal creation, follow-up, and data entry—these belong to AI. Storytelling, negotiation, and long-term relationship building—these belong to you. When these roles are clearly defined, efficiency becomes effortless.

Once your operations are automated, the next step is **scalable personalization**. AI allows you to connect deeply with thousands without sounding repetitive. Advanced language models like ChatGPT and Claude can clone your tone and brand style, ensuring that every message feels personal. Sentiment and behavioral analysis ensure your communication aligns with each client's mood, context, and preference. This balance of scale and sincerity is the mark of a master. Your outreach doesn't feel mass-produced—it feels tailor-made.

The hallmark of an AI sales empire is **self-optimization**. Every great system should learn, adapt, and improve without constant input. Predictive analytics, A/B testing, and reinforcement learning can now teach your sales engine to evolve automatically. When a certain phrase converts better, your AI remembers it. When a client segment stops responding, it experiments with new angles. Over time, your business develops what can only be described as sales intuition—an algorithmic understanding of how your customers think and buy.

But mastery extends beyond numbers—it includes **culture**. Whether you work alone or manage a team, your AI ecosystem should reflect human-centered values: trust, transparency, and empathy. Automated systems must enhance—not erode—the human experience. Every interaction should make the client feel understood, respected, and supported. You can program AI to follow up, but you must teach it to care. By designing automations that celebrate client milestones, send handwritten-style notes, and deliver genuine gratitude, you ensure your business scales without losing its soul.

Finally, the ultimate stage of mastery is **freedom through systems**. The true purpose of automation isn't to make you busier—it's to buy back your time. When every component of your sales process functions intelligently, you can step away and still grow. Your business becomes a living asset—an ecosystem that thrives independently while reflecting your mind, values, and creativity. AI gives you not just leverage, but legacy.

To achieve AI sales mastery, remember this equation: **Automation + Data + Empathy = Sustainable Scale.** Automation ensures efficiency. Data ensures precision. Empathy ensures longevity. Together, they form the foundation of a sales empire that not only generates revenue but builds relationships that last.

The future of sales belongs to those who see technology not as a threat, but as a partner. In mastering this partnership, you don't just win more deals—you change what selling means. You move from persuasion to service, from transaction to transformation.

"The Empire That Ran Itself"

It was dawn when Daniel Ruiz woke to the sound of waves instead of notifications. For the first time in years, he was on vacation—his phone in airplane mode, his mind at peace. Yet somewhere in the digital world, his business was fully alive. Leads were being identified, messages were being sent, calls were being scheduled, and deals were closing—all without him.

His AI systems had grown beyond assistants; they were now collaborators.

Months earlier, Daniel had decided to integrate every part of his business into one unified engine. He connected his CRM, email marketing, invoicing, analytics, and client onboarding into a single AI network. Every tool spoke to the others in real time. When a new lead filled out a form, the AI verified details, sent a personalized message in his voice, and scheduled a consultation based on availability. After the call, it drafted a proposal, generated an invoice, and triggered a personalized thank-you note once the contract was signed. What used to take him two days now took two minutes.

As his systems matured, Daniel hired a small team—but not to do more work. Their job was to improve the automations. His AI didn't just manage tasks—it coached his people, predicted outcomes, and optimized messaging strategies weekly. He became less of a manager and more of a conductor, fine-tuning harmony between humans and machines.

The shift was more than technological—it was philosophical. Daniel realized that selling had never really been about convincing anyone to buy. It was about understanding needs and aligning timing. AI had simply given him the clarity to see those patterns at scale. Every message his system sent was guided by empathy. Every automation was built around service.

One day, while walking through a quiet beach town, Daniel received a notification from his AI dashboard: *"Monthly revenue: $58,300. Client satisfaction: 97%. Automation efficiency: 94%. Would you like to review optimizations?"* He smiled and ignored it for the moment. He didn't need to. The system was learning on its own, improving outreach and refining campaigns as it went. His business had become self-correcting–an empire that ran itself, quietly, precisely, and purposefully.

Later that evening, he opened his laptop just to observe. On his dashboard, he saw a real-time flow of activity: new prospects entering the funnel, returning clients upgrading services, referral traffic increasing. But what moved him most was a message from an old client: *"Daniel, you've built something amazing. You've automated the process, but it still feels like dealing with a friend."*

That single line defined everything he had built. Technology had amplified his reach, but empathy had anchored his brand. He realized that AI mastery wasn't about algorithms–it was about alignment. Machines had given him scale, but his humanity had given it purpose.

As the sun dipped below the horizon, Daniel closed his laptop and whispered to himself, *"It's no longer about working more—it's about working through systems that never sleep."* He looked out over the water, feeling both small and infinite. His business didn't depend on him anymore—it reflected him.

That night, while he slept, his empire kept running—finding leads, nurturing relationships, and creating opportunities. And somewhere deep within its code, the system he built continued to learn, adapt, and care—just as he had taught it to.

Epilogue

The Human Behind the Machine

The world Daniel Ruiz created was more than a business—it was a blueprint for the future of work. What began as one independent entrepreneur's search for stability had evolved into a living example of what's possible when human ambition meets artificial intelligence. He had proven that automation doesn't erase effort; it refines it. AI doesn't remove humanity—it amplifies it.

As Daniel looked back on his journey—from late nights writing cold emails to leading an automated, human-centered sales empire—he realized that technology hadn't changed who he was. It had revealed who he could become. Every new system, every automation, and every insight had given him back fragments of his life: time with family, mental space for creativity, energy for health, and peace of mind that his business would continue even while he rested.

But his story wasn't just personal—it was universal. The lesson was simple yet profound: **you don't need to be a corporation to operate like one.** You don't need investors to build leverage. You don't need permission to automate. With today's AI tools, anyone with curiosity and courage can design systems that scale their income, amplify their impact, and restore their freedom.

The greatest transformation Daniel experienced wasn't technical—it was psychological. In the beginning, he believed success came from hard work. Later, he discovered it came from smart work. But true mastery, he learned, comes from *aligned work*—work that combines automation with authenticity. AI had taught him how to detach his income from his hours, but it had also reminded him that no system replaces sincerity. The best technology is invisible—it quietly supports your vision while allowing your humanity to shine.

In the modern world, AI is leveling the playing field. A solo entrepreneur can now outperform an entire sales department. A small business can market globally without a team. A single voice can reach millions, personalize every message, and close deals automatically. What once required years of trial and error can now be achieved in weeks. The question is no longer *if* AI can change your business—it's *how fast* you'll let it.

But Daniel's greatest insight came when he realized that AI's true power wasn't in automation—it was in awareness. His dashboards and analytics didn't just show numbers; they told stories about behavior, motivation, and growth. Every data point was a reflection of human psychology, not machine logic.

The AI simply revealed it faster. It showed him that success had always followed the same formula: understand people deeply, serve them intelligently, and deliver value consistently. AI just removed the friction.

He began sharing his systems with others—coaching entrepreneurs, small teams, and consultants. Each time someone applied his approach, the results repeated: less chaos, more confidence, and exponential growth. It wasn't magic—it was structure. The same structure that had once given him freedom now gave others theirs.

As the book closes, imagine standing where Daniel once stood—overwhelmed, hopeful, and determined. You already have the most important ingredients: curiosity, ambition, and imagination. The AI tools are simply the leverage. They'll write your messages, track your leads, analyze your patterns, and optimize your results—but only *you* can define the purpose behind it all.

The world doesn't need more automation for its own sake—it needs automation guided by intention. It needs businesses that scale ethically, communicate empathetically, and serve authentically. It needs creators who use machines not to replace people but to free them. That's what AI sales mastery truly means: turning data into dialogue, algorithms into empathy, and automation into art.

So where do you begin? Start small. Automate one process this week—maybe your outreach, your scheduling, or your follow-ups. Let AI handle what drains you so you can focus on what fulfills you. Then, expand. Build systems that learn, optimize, and improve on their own. Over time, those systems will become your allies—your silent, tireless partners in progress.

And as your empire grows, remember Daniel's final lesson: *freedom isn't built in the future—it's built in the systems you create today.*

The AI revolution is here. But it's not about machines replacing humans. It's about humans finally reclaiming time, purpose, and creativity—by designing businesses that think, learn, and serve on their behalf.

The next chapter isn't written by algorithms. It's written by you.

www.ingramcontent.com/pod-product-compliance
Lightning Source LLC
LaVergne TN
LVHW022016200926
848481LV00007B/2413